The Beasts That Guide Us Home From Memory

Sean Lause

Cyberwit.net
HIG 45 Kaushambi Kunj, Kalindipuram
Allahabad - 211011 (U.P.) India
http://www.cyberwit.net
Tel: +(91) 9415091004
E-mail: info@cyberwit.net

Printed at Thomson Press India Limited.

"I sit astride life like a bad rider on a horse. I only owe it to the horse's good nature that I am not thrown off at this very moment."

Ludwig Wittgenstein

Acknowledgements

I would like to thank Will Wells and Tom Beery for their helpful advice as I wrote these poems.

Poems appearing in *The beasts that guide us home from memory* have appeared in the following journals:

"Kafka lived" *Gargoyle Magazine*

"What longing is for" *The Raven's Perch*

"Lunch break" *Legacy: Down in the Dirt Anthology* Scars Publication, 2019

"The others" *Red River Review   Straylight   Two Hawks Quarterly*

"Church crows" *Earthshine*

"The grackle as invisible priest"

Wild Violet

"The bird as essential reading"

The Road Not Taken: A Journal of Formal Poetry

"Bird in the attic" *Illya's Honey   Briar Cliff Review*

"Why I prefer birds to angels"

Jabberwock Review

"Cockatiel not you" *Helen: A Literary Magazine*

"Catherine" *Studio One*

"Wanted: One cliché to replace the old woman currently feeding pigeons in our park" *Toasted Cheese*

"Kindred spider" *Poet's Expresso   The Halcyon Literary Review*

"Cat in freezing rain,"   "Bach on the radio," "Firefly—here, there," "Between the question" and ""Where is heaven?": *Lyrical Passion Poetry*

"Dark lake,"   *Haiku Harvest*

"After the rain: *Pegging the Wind: The Red Moon Anthology of English Language Haiku*

"Dick Dirt's Last Draw"   *The Dead Mule School of Southern Literature*

"Sea World escape plan"   *Bateu Struggle*

"Turtle vision"   *The Manhattan Review*

"My final Halloween"   *The Manhattan Review*

"My father was afraid of bees"

Ilya's Honey

"Happy Daze"   *The Dead Mule School of Southern Literature*

"Proteus's Answer"   *Foliate Oak Literary Magazine*

"A view from the white whale"

The Old Red Kimono Avocet

Contents

January 6th, 2021

I watch the chaos shimmer
from my television
like Martian cancer.
I hug my dog, who never
hated another dog
for the color of its fur,
or plotted to rule
the canine kingdom.
Another Beer Hall Botch,
exploding, impotent energy,
like a broken circuit,
no water changed to wine,
only one more busted
golden calf.
Their boomerang hate
returns in bullets and blood,
always, and always corrupts
the young. Here is a mother
made of rage and screams.
Her child's innocent eyes
glow with hatred
like radioactive flowers.
Those who imagine an apocalypse
light the fuse of insurrection,
as it comes, inevitably,
from a dream gone wrong.
It's all so far away
from the gentle world of this
beast, yet as near to the human
as a whispered "witch"
condemns her blind accusers.

Saeta

Saeta, song of faith and penance,
Saeta, bird of our arrowed
longing, sing to us now in our
darkest hour. Dove, end our nightmare.
Saeta bring us holy near,
clutched in your beak a bleeding rose.
Descend as light, as Paraclete,
Saeta wing us free from sorrow.
Or come among us pure unseen,
Love may come within the silence
between breaths, or drops of rain.
Dove of our singing, hear our prayer.
Saeta see what we've become,
eyes benighted by dark phantoms,
hearts poisoned with hate incarnate.
Saeta guide us back to kind.
See the mob that slew your watchman,
and replaced crucifix with noose.
Saeta they have cursed your song,
and wounded the air with their lies.
Let our pride snap like a broken
string. Saeta of longing we sing
your light, your song of all our souls.
Save us. Render us back to whole.

Kafka lived

Kafka did not die
in that coughing
sanatorium.
That was a cover story
issued in duplicate
by the control authorities
with so much to hide.
He became what he imagined,
a waiter
in Palestine.
He arrived incognito
though everybody knew.
The Kafka Restaurant,
where, oddly, there is no waiting,
except for K.,
who waits and waits and waits,
at last at home.
He stands officiously, watching all,
making the peas feel their guilt.
His eyes still swim in sadness,
though still, nevertheless, you
won't get past his pen
that takes your order dutifully,
painfully set down
forever.
He wears no uniform.
In fact, he's nude,
although, to be fair,
no one notices.

His customers, in identical black suits,
nod, satisfied, fulfilled, as he fills
and refills their soup, as they drink it
through their wise and thirsty beards.

He ladles a river
of lovingly silent kosher clams
on reasonable china,
a breath away from doom.
So much food and food,
humped in steaming armfuls.
Franz keeps forever feeding.
Later, he will sleep,
breathing softly,
curled in the embrace
of dozing giraffes
and the tails of animals
no one has ever seen,
with violin music
strung from the stars
like a distant memory,
just perfected enough
to make him dream
of crawling to heaven
on broken wings.

The others

A cat approached me
with a note on her paw
that read "cat."
That was sound advice,
made more sense than my "philosophy,"
yet still I craved for more.
So dragonfly came:
"I knit past to present
faster than the mind can see."
Spider whispered:
"I weave death from sunlight,
and I am the silence the grass keeps."
"Let me fold you in my breath of leaves,
called the oak,
shedding its blood in the darkening winds.
And the icicles:
"We are the moonlight melting into Spring,
and we share your tears of longing."
Too many things forever speaking!
So I hid within the night,
but there the planets ripened into meanings.
I could not shut out life.
Even in the subway
a moth lowered her sunglasses
like Audrey Hepburn and said:
"Why did you invite us here,
if you thought that you alone
was all you need?"

What longing is for

Every wind aspires to silence,
and silence for a word to contain it.
The word longs to awaken its joy,
joy for a sadness to deepen it.
My heavy feet long for the swallow's flight,
my voice for its bright silver whistle.
The swallow's flight longs for the emptiness
that the bend of its wings displaces.
Wings long to sail past storms,
the storm for an end to rages.
This world and I long for each other.
I spread my arms to let it blow through.
But what does longing long for?
For an end to longing, and a begin.

The thrill of the transient

The fleeting know time—
near as a whispered wish,
lost as the summer of dreams.
Let it be fleeting,
the electric trill of the cicada,
the firefly engoldening and gone.
Let it be random,
the windowpane blue,
then bursting with sudden angels
Elected by chance or grace,
a heaven will not be held.
Let it live and die together—
your midnight passion stars,
or meteor that burns to longing,
then plunges into mystery.
The night accepts all comers.
Surrender to joy that thrives
at the far end of somewhere,
as the moon ripens into light,
then gently hides her faces,
one by one by one....

Lunch break

I'm boothed tight at Captain D's,
poking at my Filet O'Fish—
The noise is bone-bending—
platters, clatters, and jackal laughter,
numbers yelled—I'm 43 (my age)—
Jesus, it's like they are all eating one giant
oyster, synchronized gormandizing.
Like Bloom among the Laestrygonians,
I just can't force one bite.
Clock says 12:40—It's time—it's time—
and now a winged shadow (black angel?)
rides the traffic down 309,
strange as neon in daylight.
A vulture!
Strayed here from the reservoir,
his longed-for target meal
a crunched possum on the dividing line.
He circles and circles, following his shadow.
I watch transfixed as he—lands—a car!—
rises—lands again—a truck!
He lands and flaps and hops and flies.
He can't catch a single break.
Not one sweet bite of death.
Now I realize I'm devouring my food,
my plastic knife stabbing like Ahab's harpoon,
but I'm watching that shadow, that circling
black cross, I am flesh, I am fish.
This is my body.
And then with one last pendulum swoop,

he snatches the possum on his talons,
then curves, arcs, soars toward home.
My pen is out—The time!—The time!
Writing and writing an endless hunger.

Bird lights

Inside each bird is a light.
The light is singing.
It sings of distances
between breath and silence.
At night it perches,
wondering back at what it sang by day.
And only then are its distances achieved,
its fear folded in the sleep of wings,
and its loneliness cast to a million stars.

Church crows

Here are glistening crows
that perch on the dragon heads
of the Catholic church on Market.
The bells bong—and—startled—
they fly around and around the
steeple, like black wounds in the air
curving, carving the winds with
wings and cries, exiled by God
from eternity into time.
They always return, strutting their wings.
Traffic horns, swears and whistles
of business below do not stir them.
The dragons are their home, but
the bells send them out to their
wheels within wheels, over and over again
they stay the Winter, steal their food,
and call to the sleeping dragons.
Consider the faith of crows.

The grackle as invisible priest

They possess nothing but two noises—
one a skeleton clacking upstairs,
the other a shriek that feels like wounds.
What heartless god cursed this summer bird
with such a hue and cry?
They descend like black angels expelled
from heaven, and land like an affront,
croaking the rudeness of the blinding sun.
Who clothed them in this inky cloak
then cast them unsponsored through the air?
Two clash over some discarded scraps,
lock beaks tight on each other's throats,
then tumble through the dust like cowboys.
Their thirst must wait for distant storms—
Why no bath, no house to succor them?
Every hiding place should be green, cool green.
But they must hide themselves in shadow.
Targets of cruel slingshots, ignorant stones.
Heat and indifference would have them all dead.
Why should bright colors shun them like a shame?
Only at night are they safe from pain.
A silent symphony draped through the trees,
a misericord from an absent ruler.
By midnight they are invisible priests,
praying for a dawn to end their hunger.

The bird as essential reading

A bird is essential reading
for those who need to dream,
for a bird learns wing wisdom
from a scattering of winds.
A bird is essential reading
for the text of an escape,
for a bird knows wall is illusion
and flight a new way of seeing.
A bird is essential reading
for the prisoner of plans,
so he may learn the earth seems bound
in the kingdom of the blind.

Cockatiel not you

Cockatiel,
not you,
a yellow and orange
assertion.
Bright with her own meanings,
clatters round the outside
of her cage, without fear,
flourishing her freedom.
Her eyes, seeds of darkness,
see all that is not
you, see you too, see
dual worlds, one on each side,
her head a ball turret,
tail a trailing spear,
feather in her cap.
She whistles "Whataru?"
won't wait for an answer,
explores the floor,
foraging as she goes,
Mounts the top of an armchair
renowned for its emptiness,
spreads her wings and sings
her triumph, not yours.
Outside the wide window,
madness screams in the trees.
But she sings and sings, so expertly,
the madness is not yours.

The electric chicken

Roadside stop, hovering in the Smokies,
gas, magazines, candy and a menagerie
of the captured—waterless aquariums
a-shiver with demented green lights,
a snake unwinding a tale, roach farm,
a tarantula trying to climb the invisible,
falling back like a cureless wound, legs
swirling, a clutch of mice staring at that snake
like a tiny pink apocalypse, a drain circled
with tiny mouths, an air of smothered angels.
And one chicken in a glass booth,
watching wide-eyed as my mother drops
dime after dime into its thankless home.
"Look! She dances!" she joys to my Old Man,
who shakes his head with all the woes of time
and tells her the truth: The chicken wire beneath
the bird is electrified.
My mother transforms. Her face molds a fist
of pain and her tears are knives. She seems
to grow with each step as she confronts
the owner, who squats before a tiny b&w t.v.,
his face like a thumb or a bottled fetus.
He merely shrugs and says: "It's Ma business."
Sweet Jesus, now she's overturning all the tables,
freeing all the exhibits—snakes, mice, roaches,
and birds, birds, birds! Now she's after that
electric chicken, clawing at the lock and sobbing.
The chicken nods quick encouragement like a
death row inmate at Sing-Sing in a
grade B gangster flick.

Here comes the owner! I know he's going
to gut us all and stuff us into separate
exhibits to entertain the Pilgrims of Boredom.
"Don't mess with Ma business!" he growls
around his cigar.

But my mother has somehow busted that lock,
and the whole family—Mother, Father, Son and
Holy Chicken—go tumbling out the door to our car.
The owner follows with a wide waddle, shaking his
fist and calling "Ma business!" The snake behind him
imitates a question mark. My mother clutches her prize,
her fingers quivering with all the world's violations.

Wanted: One cliché to replace the old woman currently feeding the pigeons in our city park

She feeds pigeons, only pigeons.
If a sparrow alights on her big cigar,
she blows smoke in its face
and flicks it away. And her laughter
stings the air like bees.
She snarls obscenities at perfect strangers
for not being stranger enough.
She kicks children who step too close
with her plastic Family Dollar sneakers.
She has her bench and will not budge.
The pigeons flock to her, only to her.
They are filthy and will not frighten.
Some have disturbing pink eyes,
and these birds dance occult
computations in the snow.
She appears to have a large supply of bread.
Still, she might be homeless,
which is bad for tourism,
and which may very well embarrass
some of our Christian brethren.
She refuses to give her name.
The police are baffled. She feeds and feeds,
chuffing away on her cigar. One pigeon
sits on her head like a dubious divinity.
At night she fades into shadowed trees.
A group of concerned citizens

is seeking a little old lady to replace her.
Must be neat and clean, and adore children.
Non-smoker preferred. Benefits include
nursing home accommodations if necessary.

Why I prefer birds to angels

Both are messengers,
yet birds delight
with a sudden alight and gone,
while angels bring doom and crucifixion,
and there's never one there when you need it.
Angels clasp ennui's eternity
while a bird trespasses time,
breathless as the o in wonder,
its pause between wind and wing
invisible.
Too much white seems sinister—
a blank page or mind.
I prefer crows, whose cries are wounds,
who descend like swirling nightmares,
and bruise the air in flight.
Angels watch, and watch, and watch,
fruitless guardians of the poor.
I prefer the owl, who glows right through you,
who questions the darkness,
and knows the hideouts of his meals.
They never stop beating at heaven, these birds,
forever seeking the depths of night,
or the blue within the blue.

Colors of the spirit

I cannot touch it,
this wren's bright song
as it protects
the supernatural
from the low haunts of men.

The dead undying bird

The cat has gotten at it, this tiny bird,
and now it hides its wounds below the porch.
The boy crouches, listens. The cat has
gone yet still creeps through the boy's
veins, stalking his heart to silence.
He tosses stones at the bird, one, two-
to end its pain, yes, but also to become
the cat forever, stealthy and unafraid.
He claws his arms and chest until they bleed,
while the bird sings death.
Now the boy shivers, and begins to sing
softly, gently to himself, the death song
which creeps through his veins to bind his love,
and earth and sky, so briefly, speak mercy,
the dead undying bird within his heart.

The Albatross speaks of Baudelaire

He was beautiful and wrong.
I like to smoke, to walk recklessly
among the drunken and happy men,
even when they taunt me with their game.
My flesh is not good to eat.
They must covet my vast heart
when I soar beyond all curse and vesper,
my flight a silken thread of light.
My sunken eyes whisper them visions
they long to embrace in the grace of dreams,
but the flights are long, cold and dangerous,
the ancient night wounded with stars.
Soon the ship below is long forgotten,
eyes of iron, cross of doom.
Let me go, you who bleed in words.
You will never find the language of the wing.

Air vent

There was an air vent, old and cool,
at the back of my third grade classroom,
next to my desk. Birds nested there,
calling to me from windy depths,
singing to me of other worlds,
of snake charmers in the clouds,
and a narrow path to all that blue.
Freed from the bleating teacher,
freed from the demented blackboards,
I sang quietly to my birds,
safe from the heartless numbers,
safe from the rulers and the ruled,
their nest woven around their eggs
and around my hidden world.
I returned, years later, teacher-less,
the building gone, the past embracing silence,
the song dispersed to surrounding trees,
no purity safe from loss or flight.
My birds had escaped the world
by entering it. All that remained
was memory, and my whistled praise
for all that is secret and shared.

Kindred spider

Design
the dew knows
and signs,
sudden in light,
then gone.
In moonlight,
silverblue
strung between stars,
at dawn,
a golden target in the green.
Spider
web
net of thinking,
lined
like an old woman's face.
The spider's legs move
like silent syllables.
She dances down her lines
like a breath
down a nervous question.
Shivering peace,
silent war,
and what it means
the wind knows,
winding through our dreams.
So much
depends upon
how skillfully she conjures
death, weaving it gently
into life.

Night spider

Each night
a spider spun the stars
over my bed
protecting
or capturing,
I never knew
how
it unwound the constellations
each night
sky
begun anew.
Her web cradled
all the light,
threaded the darkness
into a question:
Are stars woven from darkness,
or darkness from the stars?
It never seemed to matter
to her,
as she lowered each night,
crept through my eyelids,
and settled down to sleep within my heart.

The girl who became a butterfly

Butterfly—
wrapped in night beneath the moon,
prayed for the word to set her free.
Who but she could ever know
this loneliness furled in waiting,
this thirst for light in a dark cocoon?
Angel of color, of earth and sky,
teach us the beauty you never knew
until you learned to alight the world,
until you unfolded into love.

Precision of cricket

The sheer accuracy
of this cricket's call
is almost unendurable,
the way it ticks the time of darkness
with a perfect precision of sound,
and slowly, slowly, near dawn,
a pulse, a pulse,
then silence and alone.

Night walk

Cricket stars,
moon soul,
I never knew till now
reflected here
in this back alley
riddled in puddles,
like an old man walking a cane.
The stars call light
to darkness,
over and over in sighs,
but the night says only
shhhhhhhh…
while Venus and Mars become
a cat's eyes on a fence.
and bats scribble the air,
a sentence without beginning or end.

On the theory that light is woven from bees

It is difficult to generalize
about bee origins. No single
proposition appears to belong.
However,
this bee alights
this clover
with sound and color, burnished gold
and hum of earth, legs moving
like a typist's fingers
spelling a magic incantation.
I've forgotten the question.
But when this bee departs,
he plunders the air with freedom.

La colmena

These bees…
how their hive hums!
Like the long labors of men
in the coal mines I remember
years ago,
how they burrowed darkness,
carried light,
servants and warriors
who knew the gold they made
would never be their own.

Twelve haiku

Firefly—here—
there—advertises himself.
He's open all night.

She loves you
yeah, yeah, yeah—
Beatle Cicadas.

Bach on the radio.
A spider weaves her web
with furious joy.

Ghost on the stairs?
Only a firefly
trying to find home.

A Fall mosquito
threads the lace curtains
searching for a mate.

Perched on a leaf,
nibbling the moon—
praying mantis.

Dark lake,
the only sounds—my breaths,
ducks nibbling the weeds.

Between the question
and the answer,
the mourning dove's call.

The butterfly
easily flew
over heaven's gate.

Cat in freezing rain—
first is breath,
then its cry.

After the rain
a spider
weaving suns.

Where is heaven?
The flowers point
in all directions.

Hidden voices

The butterfly

Fewer
and fewer of us.
We don't know why.

The praying mantis

What is prayer
but hunger
gently waiting?

The earthworm

I hear
the silence
between drops of rain.

The wild duck

Watch me
drown
the wound.

The firefly

I alone
know the limits
of perception

Deer-haunted through the Alice woods

Deer-haunted through the Alice woods,
love is the all-embrace of silence.
Whispers seek where wisdom hides,
and a child escapes the wound of names,
and need not fear a ruinous Queen.
Deer-haunted through the Alice woods,
secrets from a magical mirror
tell a fawn's reprieve from fear,
where a single word spells time's return,
and the end of Summer's dreams.
Deer-haunted through the Alice woods,
no judgements, for now, may enter,
no writing desk, no raven, no need
to change the subject, a haven
where Alice guides the Knight of Innocence.
Deep within bewildered trees,
neither here nor there, we are one
as prisoners are one in darkness, till
the King wakes and we are alone again,
deer-haunted through the Alice woods.

Moose rescue

The fireman:

The thing got stuck in the ice.
It would have drowned.
We tried the safety rope
on the truck, got nothing.
Stupid thing was so big
we had to call in the
helicopter. Tranked it,
tied it tight, then air-
lifted it back to the woods.

The moose:

The earth longed for my return,
for like the air it needs my strength
to live. But an angel carried me
through the antler of the stars to heaven,
that loved me more. Finally, I
returned, for the angel knew my flesh
outweighs its spirit, and my breaths
contain its own, my legs made
for power, hunger, my blood holier
than its emptiness, my vision
more complete, for I can fall,
and rise, and return to earth
again, without ever leaving home.

Cow tipping

The cows hear them coming
long before they stagger through the field,
the lowing cows that punctuate the hill
under the lowering harvest moon.
The college students do not know
you cannot tip a cow
any more than a cow
can jump over the moon.
The cows know these creatures
come and go, come and go,
leaving nothing behind them
but curses and mockery and moons.
The cows lie calm and gentle
in the long grass, and the moon
is the earth's last candle,
refusing the darkness till dawn.

Catherine

It was the screaming
took him whole,
that second day,
Abraham, my godly man,
his faith shot all to pieces…
The wounded were strung
across the wheat field.
As death came near,
the human cries grew bestial,
the horses' cries near human.
On the third day we screamed together
through the cannons dueling for the earth.
But he continued after, screaming
through silence as I held him,
screaming at the empty air.
The Fourth was the worst.
All day he watched them bury
the Rebels in wide trenches, some hands
and eyes still uncovered in the moon,
while the still living begged for death.
That day my Abraham went silent.
After they took him, I wrote
for compensation:
"32 acres grass, 27 acres wheat,
16 dead horses. My husband, Abraham
Trostle, taken to an asylum."
I no longer know
which is worse,
the screaming
or the silence.
Somehow they are both the same.

Angel of horses

The horse,
sensing the storm
with its ears, eyes, blood,
with its dark soul,
relinquishes a cry
not of fear
but warning to the others,
and to all who will listen.
He stamps his hoof
shakes his mane
to rattle the moon awake,
paces round and round
the other horses,
weaving them to a calm,
while distant lightning
shivers the stars.
What angel
descending
to uncertain shepherds
in the cold
ever guarded innocence so rare?

My love came riding on a red, red horse

For my son, Christopher

My love came riding on a red, red horse,
released from night's grasp, racing,
relentless breaths and beat and sweat
that burst in sudden passions of the sun
and hope and gasp and thrust and cry.
Through dawn's ripped mask I heard
hoof beats pound down distant sands,
smelled the wake of you, the sweet waves
of you that rolled their manes in pride
of all things relentless and pure.
My blue-peering bundle of boy,
these words cannot hold you enough.
But this night the crows danced in joy,
ecstatic spiders spun the stars,
and your hand swept the moon through my heart.
The past is a child that awakes unseen,
eyes curious as dandelions before a breeze,
this sudden hand clenched round my finger
undoes me and anoints me father,
who holds you now as he once held me.
Now trust your horse of love to guide you home.
Cling to this flesh that beats the hourglass shore.
We are born apart, torn apart,
but something in our lightest touch
endures.

There is more mystery yet.
I will walk always before you
chanting peace to Arabian dawns,
remembering faith once cupped in palms,
and love more deep than silence.
Look!
Where horses leap the courthouse clock,
where streetlamps regard eternity.

Nietzsche's horse

Why does he hold me,
this broken man?
No one touches me
except to beat me, break me.
Doesn't he see?
All are beaten and broken
except for the masters.
Does he seek a meaning
behind these blows?
I am what they are—
They are me, my bones speak,
these bones that long
to escape my skin. Why
does he cry for me?
My master beats me when he needs me
and beats me when he doesn't, beats
me when I can and beats me when I can't—
His blows never falter, never forget.
Who is this man
who cries for the way things are?
Now the master whips him too
as he clutches my neck,
whispers in my ear
words I can never know.
But even the master does not know
the secret I'll die to keep:
That in my dreams I see the stars
come tumbling to final earth,
and every star a master proud,
screams in the endless silence.

Riding through a doorway in the rain

She rides free, the wind, wing-
sanctioned, embraces her wonder
at the coming next, her soul
in motion with the world,
her legs clenched tight—
mane, neck, flanks, tail
and girl one pure energy,
ghost breaths pluming a single freedom.
The swing and surety of stride
as she outpaces her mind towards the new,
the sun hidden in awe of what dares
outrace it, of all who find the mastery
of the wind and the reins.
Powerswift without and within,
and rhymed with the pulse of earth
she comes, hoofbeats thundering
through her bones as she—soars!—
through a doorway in the rain.
While in her eyes—a paradise
she keeps locked through all time
and time undone—a sense of
something forever leaping—
as she bursts through the blossom of the sun.

Happy Daze

I long for the authentic,
in a world gone all wrong,
and so I come to Happy Daze
to wind myself in memories.
A double decker, fries and shake,
Elvis and Buddy on the juke,
roller skating waitress brimming
with cherry cokes in the sweet notes of love.
Ads for toothpaste and deodorant,
and everything shining and clean,
white floors, white, white walls.
Nothing breaks here, not even hearts.
Inside I commune with innocence.
Outside a vague world shifts its gears.
While my breath lasts I am free of time,
guarded by stainless napkin angels.
I admire the details of this brilliant
imitation, and till we meet again,
pass a framed photograph of Trigger,
stuffed and poised for immortality.

Nirvana cat

I squat in the sun,
seeking satori.
My back aches. A tree buzzes.
A small itch creeps up my neck.
I open my eyes in tearful rage.
My orange cat purrs in the grass,
eyes closed, already in heaven.

My father was afraid of bees

My father was afraid of bees.
I used to see him run from them,
cursing, arms up like surrendered
peasants in old newsreels,
pursued by grinning bayonets.
Bats did not bother him.
He'd pick them up like big black pancakes
and fling them winging out the door
till they caught the night sky and stuck
there, exiled and perplexed.
But bees—knitting dooms of light.
Something about the needle in you, in you,
probing the skin, dancing along the pores,
listening patiently for veins, weaving round
the house, bumping windows, wanting in.
He could hear the whole hive
beating its painful beauty across broken fields,
searching for blood, spouting hypodermic malice
in sudden descents. Often I saw
how his eyes stun.
I'd follow him to the post office,
pursued by fists of raging bees,
watch him peer hunger into the honeycombed
boxes, hands dripping expectation,
but all he pulled out was handfuls of dead bees.
And whenever he tried to say
a word he longed to say,
the bees would burn from his eyes
and explode from his mouth

to keep him from love or comfort.
And when he tried to run home,
old bees would whirl round his knees
like leaves that can't remember,
covering the earth in wasted honey,
his own private carpet of loss.

If I had owned the skill,
I would have built him mighty wings
to soar above his wounds.

Coyote vision

1.
At dawn
the coyote is
a shadow within a shadow.
2.
At sunset
the coyote is
a stencil on the sky
3.
At midnight,
the coyote calls to lonely constellations
who have forgotten their names.
4.
The edge of the moon
is a blade
down which the coyote travels.
5.
The coyote's breath
under the cold stars
is the ghost of ancient hunger.
6.
Under the coyote's paws
the ice
is a poison of jewels.
7.
Sensing danger,
the coyote slips through a crevice
between the unreal and the real.

My final Halloween

Inside the mask, I was my own haunting,
true horror, the kind you dread to show.
Disguised as werewolf, hunted by the moon,
blinded by Venus but guided by Mars,
I bit my sweet lips to blood.
The mask bit each time I breathed,
and turned each breath to outraged spittle,
my eyes sunken stars, blind holes
in the mask of God, who cursed me
in the dark, nailing my tongue to words.
I had no word for my rage but howl.
I knew the candy was poisoned, the apples
blooming with razor blades, and did not care.
I had become my monster and was pure,
chased through demented woods by peasants.
Back, far back in origins, the night
crouched, waiting for its chance.
My haunted house followed me like a pet
and whole world titled on the horizon
the night my secret monster was unmasked.

Proteus's Answer

On this shore I am lord of answers.
I have preserved all my monsters
in the dark depths of vision,
safe from the pride of pirates.
The way they rob you
is to make your body a mystery,
like a stranger that follows you
wherever you go.
If you wish your body to be your own,
embrace me until you find yourself
in every bird and beast I become.
They are your body, terrible and pure.
The dove's dream of heaven,
the snake's coiled cunning,
shark's dark hunger, goat's lustful beard—
Hold on for dear life as I flow
in and out of the grasp of death.
On the homeless sea you are child and mother,
your soul coiled tight within the other.
until you let the wind follow
its own ghost home,
and your mind will become a mirror
that reflects what fools cannot see.
If you can wrestle me into truth,
you will feel good news in your blood,
snatch your prize and set me free.
The sea, strong lover, will be yours.

A view from the white whale

I thought I recognized him,
the whale-line man, when he
pricked that pin in me,
my ancient wounds maskless,
that barbaric white leg
carved from my brother.
Yet I could not understand
what he was saying. His voice,
small and far away. I must have pulled
him down with me to my
wall-less depths. Even his cannibal ship
was a sigh in the round infinite.
I returned to the vortex,
my home, the eternal silence,
sole answer to his doubloon words.
Perhaps now, wrapt in the
mingled threads of the ocean floor,
his bones will see more clearly.

Caliban's victory

We caught him when he drowned his dreaming books,
star-wound man, wrapped in himself.
—From behind, where all good treasons grow.
—From beyond, where happy endings never go.
Tyrant, he fed my thirst salt water,
clapped me devil, deformed slave, spat sharp bile
on my scaly gabardine,
did beat me and curse me beast;
words do howl and bite and hate me still,
forgetting I, a king, outrank him.
Time took me my careful plotting.
Beware the tortoise outlive you all.
His daughter took me willing.
Her man played only that chess.
I won her, and soothed her hair back
with tumbling song and all the beauty
I kept from sleep, on the cursed rock.
I loved her for the shipwrecks in her eyes.
And she did love me, did kiss my wounds,
till I turned beast, drunkard, man, king, all—
And you, spinner of words and worlds,
we'll make you a meal to stuff a gullet full.
Hunger tames all vile offenses,
and I am the darkness I call mine.
My island, mine,
where I am again mine own king.
Freedom. High-day! Freedom! Free!
No I go eat my dinner.

The secret dinosaurs

Once, I hid them in the basement,
safe from traffic and tornadoes,
their unexpected Eden,
protected from extinction,
and filled with all things fanged.
But all along the lovely beasts knew
their time was on all wrong,
and their terrible beauty could never survive
that other world of watches and wars
that loved the triumphs of puny men.
When the time came they gathered and sang
their goodbye to all that was reckless and pure,
their long necks longing for the stars
that clung to the night like jungle eyes.
I saved as many as I could,
secreting them in snake holes and tree roots,
hurling handfuls of the swimmers
finning down the local reservoir,
but most just crumbled in my palms.
That left the huge, unholy monstrosities
trapped in time like aging poets,
susceptible to blood and meteors
yet determined to endure till the end.
The pterodactyl spread her wings
then folded into flame,
but the stegosaurus, with two brains,
neither one intimidating, just froze
on Main Street, hoping no one would notice.
The slow, lumbering diplodocus,

with her throat that spanned the zodiac,
impersonated a terminal moraine.
The ankylosaurus became a rock pile,
the T-Rex a senator.

Only those who crept inside
the shadows of rolling storms
still felt the power and joy
of the world that dreamed them into birth.

Dick Dirt's Last Draw

This is the life, writer man,
my world, your words.
Write me up good.
Richard Terra, Terror
of the Wild West—just
tell the truth, kid.
About the time I shot
all them buffalo,
six million, all by myself
they say, though I'm
too modest to affirm
of deny.
And all them Mexicans I killed.
Welcome to Heaven!
Best town this side of Tombstone.
The roulette wheel is fixed,
the whisky pure nitro. The bank
is a cinch, the dice are loaded.
The Indians? Gone for good.
Upstairs is paradise,
true love for a price.
The Sheriff blew town with the school marm.
The dealer's a preacher,
the suckers lose everything.
It's all wide open, see?
I've got spies everywhere,
just in case of a ringer.
Still, it's endless fun.
Just keep your back to this wall.
Trust no one at all,
and watch out for——

Sea World escape plan

Same old shark, same old shark, same old
shark whirled round, and yet
if you could press your hand through glass
you would greet your bones pulling back
and watch your scream sink deep to silence.
Miraculous and absurd, wound
round in emotionless motion,
a snowglobe of fish and reflection.
They stare, we stare, you stare, I stare…
A ring of the trapped and barely living
turns round and round in tinted green,
smell of salt and Sulphur,
stagnant well of everlasting nowhere.
They come again, pulled by invisible
baited threads, the fish in wands of pied
insanity, a huge turtle steering for lost
constellations, shark's mouth an open wound.
This mirror involves us in indecision,
longing for stars to call us to freedom,
dreaming of heaven rivers draped in light,
and planets ripe and pure enough to eat.

Seashell

Pull the seashell
from this poem,
and sound its song
through your heart and breath
within the silence
of its question
how, or why
the soul becomes sand,
words whirled
to music
without, within,
weaving the night
to stars
and sea winds
a song
forever
your mind
in the zodiac of fate,
world within world,
a labyrinth, the flesh,
delicate, vulnerable
binding the universe,
the poem
returned to this sand,
where a single grain
begins eternity.

Turtle vision

She moves through the fluent grass
with her un-Platonic waddle,
knowing there never was
a First Idea of Turtle,
only a festoon of turtles
tied mouth to tail through the possible
green, and all is well.
Her back, wide as a pancake,
granite to the predator,
centers her world in complete turtle.
Her eggs are gold and white,
smooth sun and moon, clenching
tight their turtle eternities.
By day, she meditates the earth
to a round swoon, a self-contained silence.
She beholds all opposites
clasped whole in turtle passion.
She glows in her testudine joy
like a Tiffany lamp with feet,
pleased with her own enlightenment.
By night, her ebony eyes
behold the sky curved round with turtles,
strung with turtle gods and angels,
and below, turtles all the way down.
A great turtle grunt announces
a new music of the spheres, each sphere
enshelled in the sweet bell of the universe.
And she asks you:
"What is heaven if not here,

where what I see
in my bright imagery
is all and only what I am,
and what I am is sum of all I've seen
in my patient, tortoise journey?"

Moon of the hidden world

"The Autumn moon!
leaning against the veranda post
and moving round it."

Shofu-ni

What was it like
to watch that moon circle you
with all the stars pulled round
while you in turn move round,
a moon to a moon,
the worn wood smooth down your back?
The earth alone unturning,,
such a center of all love,
you'd think it would have ended all the wars.
Perhaps I felt this once,
when I would perch on the center
of the schoolground merry-go-round.
You had to climb to that navel of time
on all fours, and if you made it safe,
a hidden world unspun around you.
Your mind darted in the sun
like a dragonfly, breathless as the flash
of a garter snake,
or a butterfly
inscribing all directions in the air.

My mother's secret chancel

Twelve years old, my mother
built a private chancel in the woods,
made of two trees, a wooden plank,
a candle, and her love.
She was not alone there—
Spiders wove old faces in the grass,
while bees pondered the air, circled,
alit, and burrowed to sweetness.
Oh my dear, your faith, your hallelujah:
Willows dream in willow longing,
turtles clasp whole in turtle love,
the way to the grass is through the grass,
the earth all heavens undone at last.

Los Pajaros Anidan

—Gloria Fuertes

Los pajaros anidan in mis brazos,
en mis hombros, detras de mis rodillas,
entre los senos tengo codornices,
los pajaros se creen que soy un arbol.
Una fuente se creen que soy los cisnes,
bajan y beben todos cuando hablo.
Las ovejas me pisan cuando pasan
y comen en mis dedos los gorriones,
se creen que you soy tierra los hormigas,
y los hombres se creen que no soy nada.

The Birds nest

—Gloria Fuertes

The birds nest in my arms,
on my shoulders, behind my knees.
Between my breasts are quails.
They believe that I am a tree.
The swans believe I am a fountain.
They come down and drink when I talk.
The sheep that pass, pass over me,
and perched on my fingers, the sparrows eat.
Ants believe I am the earth,
and men believe I am nothing.

(Translated by Sean Lause)

Trusting the wasps

Trusting the wasps

1.
I killed the first one
with a rolled-up *Time,*
pounding her life out
under war, murder, and disease.
When I was done
she looked like a poisoned fig,
her body riddled with seeds,
her eyes pinpricks of mystery,
my body a disheveled room
filled with wings and things undone.

2.
Now there are dozens
between my upstairs screen window
and the antique door with ivory knob.
They come and go through cracks
the size of a fingernail.
Sometimes they forget the way back,
clinging to the glass,
licorice eyes shifting up, around,
searching for a lost paradise.

3.
Have they journeyed here from outer space

to gauge my knowledge of earth?
The sun touches them black, green, bottle-blue,
ecstatic bottle-cap angels
descending like helicopters,
then whirring into maple seeds,
spinning the sun's gold,
beating to a pulse
in baseball diamond breezes,
swirling through fields of light.

4.
Faith is a mirror
which reflects what it cannot see.
Take me, then,
who knows no flight beyond dream.
If I close my eyes,
will I feel my wings
beating in sudden palms of light?
Ticking time to dust with yours?

5.
Today I opened the door,
stepped outside with a deep breath
and bare feet,
but the air was weighted with betrayals.
I long for a trust
as clean as my grandmother's linin on the line,
as pure as a child's breath,
dunking for apples
Come then,
you sly killers,

sting my mouth to life.
Death is whatever
makes us count to two.

6.

One lands in my palm.
It feels like a baby's breath.
Its legs probe my life-line.
Then it stings me, over and over.
Its rage merges briefly with my pulse.
This love is impossible.
It cannot pierce these bones of gravity.

7.

Indoors, the wasp rages against mystery,
coils up like a tip of smoke,
pounds its head blindly into windows
like a finger gesticulating points
in an argument it cannot comprehend.
I suspect it hates me,
but I mistake its rage.
It hates my walls,
my lying windows,
my confinement and flightless certainties.
I open the window
and it ascends to a freedom
it must sense in sleep.

8.

Last night I dreamed of wasps.

One leapt into my house,
hovered in my brain,
at home in the darkness,
stinging memories to life.

9.
Now I kneel naked,
open the door, reach to them.
They almost let me touch them,
then pull away as if on strings.
When I breathe deeply
they creep closer, waiting for me
to come with them over the trees,
through the net of stars,
as we drop from world to world
like the stinging tears of God.

10.
I can sit with them now, mornings,
when the cold sun stuns them sluggish.
Do not go near the nest.
Do not attempt to snatch them.
Do not flinch or show fear.
You can die.
Learn to breathe
like a child's whispered song.
The wasp awaits your finger like a ring.

11.
A dandelion is a clutch of gold coin

turning silver with the fears of Fall.

12.
Late October,
a ring of black and gold wasps watches me dress
from the window of the ivory-handled door.
They have formed a perfect circle
of skydiver hope,
each foreleg crossing its brother's or sister's,
wings folded round a bitter dawn.
I pull the door open gently
to let them in.
They drop to the floor with a whisper
like bits of finely spun glass,
then a sudden wave of wind
brushes them from my sight with a sigh.
Where?
Back to the earth they spun in dances.
Back to the depths beneath lost cities.
Back to the secret veins which coined them
from hunger in the lion's mouth.

Escape artist

The animal
had gnawed off its own foot
to escape the human trap.
My friends showed pity,
anger, even desire
for revenge on the human.
Yet how did they know
the creature, now free,
was not merely through
with the wound?

"Come forth into the light of things,
Let Nature be your Teacher."   —William Wordsworth

The beasts that guide us home from memory

That cloud,
that rose of the winds
high in the blue of memory,
when you finally
and suddenly
loved me
in the grass
written free with cricket calls,
the sun a throbbing flower
as we lay all gold and green
until the moon appeared,
an O of silver wonder,
and the beasts that guide us home from memory
watched gently from the nearing stars.